Advance Praise for A Rose in a Teacup

"Rachelle N. Rose has written beautiful poems in her collection, *A Rose in a Teacup and Other Poems*. Some of her poems include various colorful flowers, rainbows, sunsets, and the heavens. Two of the most powerful poems are "Not Long Ago," because it describes the world as it is today, and "To the Ones We've Lost" of which she writes, 'Your memory shall be our sunshine during these cloudy times.' Rose's inspirational collection is filled with hope."

—**Jenny Delos Santos,**
Author of *Falling Perfectly Without Trying*

"Let your imagination create the pictures in your mind while the words in this beautiful poetry collection do the heavy lifting of setting the scene. Make sure to grab a blanket and warm beverage, too, as *A Rose in a Teacup* will provide a perfect moment for relaxation."

—**Melissa Vigil,**
Author of *I Wish My Mom Was Here*

"*A Rose in a Teacup and Other Poems* is an exquisite and vivid journey through nature and life from the comfort of your armchair. Take it."

—**Simi K. Rao,**
Author of *Under the Shade of the Banyan Tree*

"*A Rose in a Teacup* is a celebration of positivity in a world that longs for it. Rachelle Nevaeh Rose does a deft job of breathing life into her beloved garden. From the stunning beauty of her varied roses to the sheer simplicity of the shy, oft-ignored dandelions, the poet takes the reader on a journey of vivacity and animation. Dancing, prancing, and twirling to the drum of artful personification, we observe through the lens of a variety of seasons, the relationship between flora, fauna, and nature's cycles.

Just as relative, is the attention paid to the many facets of love in our human nature. Depicted in flowing prose that wraps the reader in this universal need, we are reminded of how important it is to love and be loved. *A Rose in a Teacup* is an impressive read."

—Dallas Hembra,
Author of *Kaleidoscope* and *Shaking the Family Tree*

A Rose in a Teacup
and Other Poems

Rachelle Nevaeh Rose

A Rose in a Teacup
and Other Poems

Rachelle Nevaeh Rose

Green Bay, WI

A Rose in a Teacup and Other Poems by Rachelle Nevaeh Rose, copyright © 2022 by Rachelle Nevaeh Rose. Author photos courtesy of Nancy Varberg Photography. Cover illustration only created by Mary Scheel, © 2022 by Mary Scheel. Full cover art design, interior layout design, chapter head artwork, and the Written Dreams logo © 2022 by Written Dreams Publishing. This book reflects the opinions of the author and her life's decisions. Written Dreams Publishing does not approve, condone, or disapprove of these opinions.

All rights reserved. In accordance with the U.S. Copyright Act of 1976, no part of this publication may be reproduced, distributed, or transmitted in any form or by any means, or stored in a database or retrieval system, without prior written permission of the publisher, Written Dreams Publishing, Green Bay, Wisconsin 54311. Please be aware that if you've received this book with a "stripped" off cover, please know that the publisher and the author may not have received payment for this book, and that it has been reported as stolen property. Please visit www.writtendreams.com to see more of the unique books published by Written Dreams Publishing.

Publisher/Executive Editor: Brittiany Koren
Illustrator: Mary Scheel
Cover Art Designer: Ed Vincent/ENC Graphics
Print Interior Layout Designer: Amit Dey
Ebook Interior Layout Designer: Amit Dey

Category: Poetry, Single Author Collection
Description: Single author collection of poetry about being an innkeeper, the seasons, gardens, and real life issues.
Paperback ISBN: 978-1-951375-65-2
Ebook ISBN: 978-1-951375-66-9
LOC Catalogue Data: Applied for.

First Edition published by Written Dreams Publishing in March, 2022.
Ebook Edition published by Written Dreams Publishing in March, 2022.

Green Bay, WI 54311

Table of Contents

A Flower...1

Heaven on Earth..2

Sunshine in My Hair......................................3

White Daisy..4

Awakened Beauties..5

A Rainbow Emerges..6

Golden Wheat at My Feet..................................7

A Butterfly Journey......................................8

Little Dancers..10

Bittersweet...11

Back to School..12

A Fall Sunset Reveals the Moon..........................14

Singing Good-bye..15

Snow Angel..16

Postcard Scene..17

Granny's Christmas Tree.................................18

Waterfall...20

The Mountain's Night Sky................................22

Pearls of the Sea.......................................24

A Peaceful Destination	25
Late Night Visitors at the Lake	26
Traveling Eyes	28
A Sky Island	30
Prima Ballerina	32
Snow in May	33
Yellow Daffodil	34
Find Joy	35
Late Fall	36
Rainbow Beam	38
To the Ones We've Lost	39
A Matter of the Heart	41
Love Again	42
Love Is a Dance of the Heart	43
Love Is…	44
Gallant Lover	45
Love Out Loud	46
A Virtuous Woman Loves	47
Love and Prejudice	48
Love That Can Fly	49
Play a Love Song of the Heart	50
Heart Blossoms	51
Summer's Door	52
Courage	53

Be Kind	54
Wander	55
Optimistic	56
Dare to Dream	57
Being Me	58
Be Happy	59
The Injured Earth	60
Bleeding Hearts	62
Pink Orchid	63
Stunted Growth	64
Good Night and Good Morning	65
A Bouquet	66
Double Rainbow	67
Lovely Smiles	68
Love Gathers at the Table	69
Garden of Love	70
A Wish Garden	71
Rain	72
Fireflies	73
What Star Is This?	74
Indigo Sky	75
Life's a Celebration	76
The Rainbow	77
The Pot of Gold	78

An Explorer	80
Breathtaking	82
Summon Spring	83
Royal Tea	85
Recipe of Love	86
Smiles	87
Alarm Clock	88
Winter Cardinals	89
Life Is a Poem	91
Swans of the Lake	92
Lilacs	93
Red Roses	94
Regret	95
A Midnight Visitor	96
The Ocean Remembers	97
Chasing the Sun	99
A Cat's Melody	101
Perennials	102
Annuals	103
Red Velvet	104
Fields of Flowers	105
Scent of Lilacs	106
A New Year	107
I'm Ready	109

When Life Gives Me Lemons	111
Gems of the Northern Minnesota Sky	112
The February Sky	114
Turning Colors	115
Hot Air Balloon Rides in Stillwater	116
Sipping on Memories	117
Frozen Stars	118
Not for Sale	119
The Painting	120
The Last Snowflake to Fall	122
Trumpeters on the St. Croix River	123
Fall in Love Again at the Inn	124
A Dandelion Tale (Weed or Flower?)	125
A Rosy Cheek	126
Dreams	128
A Broken Wing	129
Blooming Passionflower	132
Maple Tree Row	134
Bittersweet Is Hidden in My Heart	136
The Best Present	137
A Winter Reverie	138
Making Friends	141
Honey	142
Solo Bird	143

Spring 144
A Lovely Red Rose 145
Seeds 146
Duckling Crossing 147
Not Long Ago 148
Summer Sky 150
Green Grass 151
Freedom Flower 152
Heartbeats 153
Peru's Rainbow Mountain 154
Morning Sunshine 155
Summer Symphony 156
Love Each Other 157
Lily Pads 158
Sunflower 159
Dance Like the Earth 160
A Rose in a Teacup 161
About the Author 165

A Flower

A flower flatlines all winter long,
jolted to life
by a thunderbolt exploding loudly.
A flower's new heart beats
and begins again
as the days pass by.

When a flower grows,
it stretches its petals
toward the steady, shining sun in May.
It toasts a brand-new day
with a tall glass of sparkling morning dew
as the sun rejoices and applauds!

In autumn,
a flower bends to kiss
the golden ground goodnight.

A flower sheds its petals
when it sleeps all winter long
beneath the maple tree,
where it dreams of lovely gardens
and the wonderful music pollinators sing—
until it comes back to life in spring.

Heaven on Earth

Each flower flirts with the thought of stardom,
the sunrises and sunsets are jealous of my garden,
because the buds are kissed by the rising sun.
They dance and twirl like ballerinas on a stage
with every breeze that comes their way.
Birds sing their praises during the day
as the flowers twinkle like stars from the morning dew,
they catch you by surprise.
The variety of blooming flowers demands the attention
of all curious eyes…
A rainbow, a medley of colors, reaches for the blue dome
of the sky,
where there are cotton clouds effortlessly drifting by.
It's easy to see each flower represents love, friendship, grace,
and purity.

Sunshine in My Hair

I picked a yellow daisy today to accessorize;
Now there is a flash of sun,
in my bun,
just the perfect size.

White Daisy

White petals wave to me in the wind, surrounding a yellow center, a full moon's glare.

My heart, in the center of a daisy, is protected by the white picket fence of petals.

My heart is full of joy, peace, and love because God planted a white daisy there.

Awakened Beauties

Long cold days passed by and seemed like an eternity,
                      a countdown to the month of May.

Budding pink roses awaken from a sleepy winter,
                      by the kiss of the sun's ray.

A vivid memory is a blink of time,
                to see the roses gasping for warm air.

I look forward to the day when they grow big enough,
                to wear in my long unruly, curly, hair.

A Rainbow Emerges

---※---

A glance at a garden is like
                            watching a rainbow emerge

The radiant pigments shine so bright,
And bloom into a beam of lovely flowers
            arched in a crescent row
                like a rainbow,
the flowers exceed the span of a rainbow…
                      as it exudes beauty when it grows.

Golden Wheat at My Feet

Fall leaves turn into colorful ashes
burned by the afternoon sun
and rest at my feet.
I see the red, orange, and brown colors
melt into the ground
and reflecting the color of golden wheat.

A Butterfly Journey

The monarch butterfly,
like a delicate orange leaf,
is picked up by the gentle wind,
tossing it higher and higher
into the crisp fall air,
sprightly reaching
heights of two miles high off the ground.

Wings are folded together
to become a sail
as it surfs the breeze
at 12 miles per hour.
Until tiny feet land
on a milkweed plant,
where it will lay 100 eggs
and die soon after…
But don't be melancholy,
the eggs will hatch
in four days and turn into
hungry caterpillars.
They will devour
their milkweed haven
until they grow plump

and spin into a chrysalis,
born into royalty,
named after
the King of Orange.

The autumn leaves
bow before them.
They conquer flower after flower,
to store up on its nectar.
Then, they fly to their southern kingdom
to embrace the faithful oyamel fir trees
until the bark radiates with orange.

Little Dancers

Autumn colored tutus
leap effortlessly across the purple sky.
They continue to twirl
when they land on solid ground.

Then, the wind picks up
and drags them across the stage,
like a prima ballerina
ending a Broadway show.

Just when you thought it was over,
they lift off the ground again
in a little tornado
to finish their full turns
and land perfectly in relevé.

They wait for your applause,
as you daydream of
dancing autumn leaves
in the cool breeze.

Bittersweet

Bittersweet is a vine with
blooming orange berries
which look
exposed in the fall months.

It is sunshine
in a vase that doesn't
require water.

Every fall, we go
bittersweet hunting.
It's a treasure
difficult to find.

It thrives
by rocky cliffs,
on hills and by trees.

When you spot these little orange berries,
the promise of autumn has begun!

Back to School

When September comes along,
children's summer vacation
comes to an end.

They'll protest like a stubborn mule
against returning to school.

Autumn has arrived,
another child has survived
the mischief of summer.

I'll be glad to see them go
because I miss smudges
on the school bus windows
as little noses
press up against the glass.

No more roaming the outdoors
looking for spaces to explore.
It's time for little
children to go back to class.

I miss each dog's tail wagging
when their little owner gets off the bus
while their mom holds him back.

On the first day of school,
each child's eyes
are filled with
excitement and surprise.

A Fall Sunset Reveals the Moon

The cobalt blue sky
makes me fix my eyes
below on the leaves.
Some remain on
the huge oak trees
as they rustle in the wind.
Colors of gold, rosewood, and bronze
melt together on the surface of the lake
as the color of the sky reflects on it,
until the sun becomes a smashed pumpkin
beneath a grey boot of a cloud.

I stay and wait until the sun goes down,
in awe of the amazing orange sunset
and wait a little bit longer for the pendant moon
to reveal itself from behind the fluffiness.
The giant moon, a golden delicious apple,
which sweetens the sky,
and the tiny stars buzz around
the ball of honey,
also known as the Autumn Moon.

Singing Good-bye

Soon the lovely birds
will sing a good-bye song.
Their little beating hearts
always in rhythm
with their warbling.
They'll sing
and flap their tiny wings to the beat.

I'll miss their morning songs
that wake me from slumber.
I'll miss them clinging to my bushes
that make me stare and wonder…
I'll miss them nesting in my trees
and above my doors and in my wreaths.
I'll miss watching their babies take flight.
I'll miss their delightful sight.

But, most of all, I'll miss the birds
that pack their songs with them.
I can't wait to see and hear them again!

Snow Angel

A red headed five-year-old girl
waited all year long
for the first fall of snow.

She played Christmas songs
and waited for temperatures to get low.

She stared out the old, beveled glass window
until finally, she saw some twinkling snow.

Snow sparkled in the evening glow
from the outside glimmering light show.

She hurried like a busy bee
and put on her boots and snow pants.

She ran outside and plopped down in the snow
and threw her arms over her head.

She'd practiced in her little bed
and pretended to flap her wings.

Then, she began to sing
Christmas songs like an angel.

Postcard Scene

As the earth tipped upside down
like a snow globe,
for a few seconds,
it created a fierce blizzard.
Even the perfect fluffy snowflakes
shivered in the cold.
You'd think that all life ceased.

There were red cardinals
in the bushes by the windows.
Snow-capped mountains
of pine trees lined the driveway.
The small cottage nestled
by the frozen lake's edge.

Every year, I collect
the scenes that in
winter appear,
perfect little postcards
mailed to my mind's mailbox.

Granny's Christmas Tree

It's Christmas eve and
the large massive pine tree
in the living room
is guarded by
nutcracker soldiers
of all different colors and sizes.

The fat family cat, Storm Cloud,
lies under the tree.
He swats at a few ornaments
and people's feet as they walk by.

Children try to pick him up
but he squirms out of their arms
until they set him down.
He's busy guarding the tree.
One child gives it another try.
Storm Cloud darts away like a fly
and runs away, knocking down
all the nutcracker soldiers.

Then he climbs the tree
bending the top slightly
as if he were the star...

He is a storm cloud,
and soon ornaments rain down
as little children frown.

A little storm surely appeared.
The puppy, Rambo, is barking near,
at the grinch of a cat.

Storm Cloud grabs ribbon from below
and tugs it in a circle,
which turns the Christmas tree
around and around
as if it were a merry-go-round.

The cat falls to the ground
and runs away, an ornament
hooked on his long gray tail.

The tree has seen better days
but it is the most memorable
of Granny's large, precious
Christmas trees!

Waterfall

The sound of a waterfall
is like a thousand waves
crashing all at once.
Like lace on a long train
of a wedding dress.

White water pours
down below into the river
where an immense
seafoam green
swimming hole awaits.

The water races over
large, smooth rocks
on the edge of a cliff.
It doesn't slow down
or stop for anyone.

A vibrant rainbow emerges
where the mist meets the sunlight.
The waterfall is the backdrop
of a mental snapshot.
The green of the wild jungle

surrounds it and tries to guard it
from being discovered.

It's too late…
I'm the first to jump in the
cold, refreshing water.

The Mountain's Night Sky

The large, winsome full moon
is a flawless ivory pearl orb
begotten from omnipotence and perched high.

The myriad of stars
are sparkling diamonds scattered, chiseled, and dangling
from the exquisite dazzling, black onyx sky.

The night sky is a jewelry box.
There isn't a key or a lock.
Striking stars steal the free show.
They twinkle and brightly glow
like white daisies without a stem.
Look, before the clouds hide the floating gems.

During the quiet of the night,
the mountain sleeps without a fight
and shows off the jewels of the sky.
If they could teach me how to fly
I, too would be a gem in the sky
with a twinkle in my eye
from joyous tears I would cry.

Nothing above the mountain's peak is more serene
except the reason why stars mysteriously gleam.

I'm paralyzed by the luminous display.
I don't want dawn to steal it away.

Pearls of the Sea

A mountain of waves
push forward and burst
over the lovers of the sea,
letting in a grain of sand,
a flash of light,
a vivid memory
settling into our hearts.
It forms a precious pearl,
a hidden treasure inside,
which can't be taken.

The lovers long for
the peaceful Sun of summer,
to become one
with the rise and fall of the waves,
desiring with each breath
to keep such moments
from slipping into the sea.

A Peaceful Destination

Every year, I take a trip to the sea…
Hawaii, Costa Rica, Puerto Rico, Jamaica and Peru
are just a few places I like to go
and walk on the beach,
where I curl my toes into the sand.
I look for conch shells.
I want to hear the ocean
whenever I wish.
When I find a large one,
I put it to my ear as though
I have picked up a phone.
I don't speak.
Instead, I listen to the ocean's song
as if I've heard it for the very first time.
I find joy and peace within its song.
Time stands still.
Then, I'll look at
the fast, roaring waves
devouring my footprints in the sand
as if I wasn't there.
A new place undiscovered by little feet,
because each wave washes away
the evidence of humans.

Late Night Visitors at the Lake

The inn was nestled
on the banks of the
small lake.
I awoke to hear the words
"come with me"
whispered in my ear
and a flashlight shining
on my face.
We were off within minutes
in the blue canoe.

The full moon shimmered
across the lake.
I heard crickets and frogs
chirping in the calm
of the night.
A cool summer breeze
brushed past my face and
pushed the canoe forward
with little effort.

We saw two loons,
most likely lovers,

in the middle
of the glass top lake.
They thought they had
the stillness to themselves
until we arrived.

There was a little trail
of ripples behind them
and our canoe.
The loons cheerfully
sang their vows
before they saw us.
Then, they ran
and flapped their wings
on the surface of the water
before taking off.
They had somewhere else to be
and we had no other place
we'd rather be.

Traveling Eyes

The jagged rocks
look like stairs
leading to the top of the cliffs.
As the sky grows dark,
the mountain becomes
a Christmas tree with a big star
resting on its peak.
The bright full moon
makes my eyes focus
on this particular mountain peak.
It becomes a part of the sky
and a piece of the landscape
as if it were a puzzle
that is missing a piece—
your presence.

If you were here with me,
I'd share the view of
the top where all trees
reach for the stars,
as if they were not so far away.

I do not need to climb
to the high altitude because
I prefer to climb
the majestic mountain
with my traveling eyes.

A Sky Island

The slow floating clouds
surround a mountain peak.
The wind currents of
the deep blue above
makes the waves of clouds
dip and crash among its shore.
It is known as Sky Island
for its isolation from the
desert land below.

You'd think that nothing
could live in
the high altitude; but
that assumption is wrong.

Bighorn sheep
and some of the oldest trees have survived.
Other flora and fauna can be encountered
along the way to the top of the peak.

The wonder of the mountain
is another world mystery
of how an island can exist

at such an airy high altitude.
The panoramic vista
connects nature to a place
as if it were heaven here on Earth.

Prima Ballerina

A purple flower blooms all day
as bright as a sunshine ray.
Her presence brings a smile to my face
and makes the world a better place.

Weeds may pop up and grass will grow tall
but this flower is the prettiest at the ball.
She stretches tall like a prima ballerina twirling;
she could've had her own Broadway show.

I'll interpret the summer dance from the front row.
If she never stops twirling while she grows
and spends more and more time on her toes,
she will be a prima ballerina stealing the show.

We may know her by name one day,
but meanwhile, we admire her graceful ways
while she twirls and twirls in the wind
when the show begins!

Snow in May

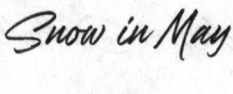

Mother Nature is confused.
She whispered words of spring
in my trusting ears…
but spewed out snowflakes
out of her mouth in a
whirlwind fashion.

The snowflakes look like
tiny, frosted sugar cookies
floating through the
cool, dense air.

Snow in May,
put on your shocking show
and then, please go away!

Yellow Daffodil

A yellow daffodil
is the rising sun.
It brightens the world,
giving gifts of life and fun!

Find Joy

Whispers of joy and
shouts of laughter
make one live
happily-ever-after.

Late Fall

The shift in weather
wasn't a smooth transition.
It rained and rained in October—
the leaves were supposed to
change colors weeks ago.

I was afraid it would snow
and that the leaves wouldn't let go.
The fall season transmutation
would soon take place.

Finally, leaves were falling to the ground
everywhere, filling every inch of space.
If I could revise fall,
I'd make it last all year long,
and embrace the cool, crisp days
with sunshine beaming.

The light beams would rest on
my wrap-around porch.
I'd sit there and enjoy every
moment, daydreaming among the
vibrant colors of the leaves

in the abundant trees.
The official send-off as
they wave good-bye
before winter comes
with its icy breeze.

Rainbow Beam

The arched rainbow beam
purposely brightly gleams
so one can admire the earth's beauty
for several moments of its aesthetic duty.

Its vibrant colors hover over the sea of blue
where it is suspended freely as it captures you.
Your mind could be anywhere else right now
but your attention is steady, taking a vow.

To never ignore something so alluring,
like the arched rainbow beam.
A vivid, colorful dream.

To the Ones We've Lost

Your smiles live on
in the midst of the pain
as our country mourns for you
in the rain.

Your memory shall be
our sunshine
during these cloudy times.

The storm came when we
didn't see it coming.
We stayed home and wished
for the best,
for your safety,
your survival.
All we do now
is pray for the rest.

Your smiles live on
in the midst of our pain.
Our country mourns for you
as it rains.

Your memory shall be
our sunshine
during these cloudy times.

We have not forgotten you.
With the help of God,
we will get through.
These hard times make us blue.
No one could predict this awful news.

We shall light a candle for you
on a cloudy night, so your soul
lives on and can shine so bright.
We'll plant a pretty flower
in the garden to remind us of you!

To the ones we lost…
We wanted to protect you
no matter the cost.

A Matter of the Heart

Love, not to say you once loved,
but love so you can share it.
Love someone without persuasion
for true love needs *no* persuasion.

Take a leap toward love,
for you'll be loved in return.
Love without borders,
without reservation
to expand your love
across the earth.

Love Again

My heart shall love again;
I'll find a man who agrees
with my heart's desires.
He will love who I used to be,
who I am now,
and who I'll be in the future.
Although my heart was broken,
a true love will bring sutures
and I shall heal and love again.
Then, my heart will beat
to the rhythm of his.
I deserve to be happy
and so does my love.
I shall love again
because love always wins!

Love Is a Dance of the Heart

Love is like the tango;
two hearts lure each other in.
Love is like the waltz;
it's never off beat.
Love is like a swing dance;
two hearts beat to the same rhythm.
Love is like a ballet;
it never steps on others' toes.
Love is like a mambo in the street;
it dances as though there is an audience.
It doesn't matter which dance it chooses…
true love scores a perfect ten!

Love Is...

Love is a circumspect
affection of the heart!
True love can't
be torn apart!

Gallant Lover

Seek a gallant lover
who isn't easily
frightened
by love.
Seek a gallant lover
who isn't afraid
to love you for
who you are.
We all have flaws—
both good and bad.
Seek a gallant lover
who isn't persuaded
to choose money
or fame—a blinded game,
over true love.

Love Out Loud

Those who love out loud
live and breathe love.
Then, they share it!
They don't keep it
to themselves.
That would be a waste
of a good heart.

A Virtuous Woman Loves

A strong virtuous woman loves
romantic justice of the heart.
She doesn't marry for money,
status, or the fear of being lonely.
She marries for true love's sake…
She loves with all
her heart unconditionally until it aches!

Love and Prejudice

Love isn't prejudiced.
It can happen to anyone
with an open heart at any time!

Love That Can Fly

You can't stop a bird from flying
in the same way you can't stop
a heart from loving.

Love soars
from the center of its core,
above the trees and
against a breeze.

Love flies
above the
azure skies
where its only view
is you looking up
with love in your eyes.

Play a Love Song of the Heart

A melody of the heart,
a musical utopia—
the notes will never depart
from the center of love,
a musical symphony of the heart.

Heart Blossoms

A heart fully
blossoms
when in love.
The heart beats
like steady droplets of rain.
Then, it pours a little faster
all it has into the
presence of another
heart blossom.

Summer's Door

When I walk in
my garden it's like
walking through
summer's door.
It's opened to all
who want to see
what summer is
supposed to be.
Rose bushes,
daisies, pansies,
hydrangea,
purple lilacs,
and colorful tulips all stand tall.

Come walk
through my
garden's door with me—
to experience the world so small.

Courage

Breathe out courage
of a brave lion and
look fear in its eyes!

Be Kind

Always take the time
to be kindhearted.
Reverse unkind words
in your mind
and choose
healing words to
depart from your
lips, knowing that
you can't erase
unkind words
that can pierce
a heart and soul.
But you can be kind.

Wander

I don't wander when
I'm lost.
I purposefully wander
when I'm found
so I don't follow
the same path
as the lost crowd.

Optimistic

I'll stay optimistic in
a world of pessimists.
I won't let a dark cloud
hover over me.
If necessary,
I'll create my own
ray of sunshine!

Dare to Dream

To dare to pursue a dream
of living in the face
of overwhelming odds
of rejection…
Remember, rejection itself
means you are different and
that is a worthy dream!
The more rejection letters,
the more different you are
compared to the norm.
Go ahead, turn those
letters into dreams.
Daring to dream frees
you from boundaries.
Don't leave dreams in the past!
Drag dreams into the future!
Dare to dream!

Being Me

I've learned to be me!
There is no other
who can do a
better job
at being me
than me.
I need to be me!

Be Happy

To be happy is a chore.
We need to work at it every day.
Being happy is a choice
that doesn't choose us.
We choose to be happy!

The Injured Earth

What happened to the
tiny baby tree toads
in the middle of summer?
Where did the
salamanders go?
What happened
to the hundreds of
caterpillars and
monarch butterflies?
I used to capture
them as a curious child…
I was an admirer that cherished
their very existence.
These creatures and
so many more didn't have a
fighting chance against
chemicals, pollution,
and climate change.
I detest the sludge running
off into the creeks, rills,
lakes, and oceans!
I detest the pollution
being emitted in the air

by large factories.
Earth is gasping!
My animal friends are disappearing.
Sadly, one day Earth will take
its last breath.

Bleeding Hearts

White, red, and pink bleeding hearts
fill unwanted space in the garden
with their hearts and souls.

Old-fashioned bleeding hearts
empty their love into my garden
and make it a better place to visit.

Pink Orchid

The bowed stem
of the pink orchid
streams through the air
like the tail of
a shooting star!

Stunted Growth

A seed planted in the shade
will not sprout and grow
because it is afraid of the dark.

Good Night and Good Morning

All flowers get
beauty sleep at
night.
Yes, all
gardens sleep.
The flowers are not
awakened by
the nightly frog's song
or the crashing waves
of the waterfall.
They awaken
to the command
of the sun's rays
in the morning.
They
can't pull
a shade and
ignore it.
Besides,
they simply
adore it.

A Bouquet

In the morning,
flowers suddenly
awaken and stretch
their petals toward
the warming sun.
At noon, when they
are fully awake,
they are hand-picked
for their uniqueness
and come together
for a lovely bouquet
designed just for you!

Double Rainbow

A double rainbow
is holding up the
blue sky of Stillwater
with its strength
of impeccable beauty.

Enjoy the show
before the light rain
returns and the sun
moves behind
a large cloud
and its beauty weakens.
Catch a snapshot
while it is still
awake,
before it's too late!

Lovely Smiles

They share
the comfort of knowing
their deep affinity
for each other
called true love
like a rain drop falling
in a lake; it makes
a little ripple of love,
which affects
everyone they see.

When I see them
side by side and
watch lovers
turn a whisper
into a kiss
as they walk
to breakfast
wearing beautiful smiles,
it rekindles my hope
for true love.

Love Gathers at the Table

Everyone has a heart.
He chose her heart;
She chose his.
Oh, how he loves her dearly!
He holds her hand as if they
fell in love for the
very first time every day
at the dining room table.
After exchanging glances,
it confirms theirs
was love at first sight!
Their love is woven together tight!
Their love will never unravel,
for it lives on beyond the years
through laughter and all the tears.

Garden of Love

Love is a flower that
is always in bloom at the inn!
It's a beautiful sight
to see and its sweet scent
drifts through the door
of the inn.

A Wish Garden

If I can distract your eyes
away from the sky
to gaze upon my garden…
like a firework display,
with colors bursting
in every direction.

I shall make this garden
a wish garden where people
come to make a wish upon
a sleepy, drooping flower—
a fallen star—
a reminder that
stars also exist
not too far…
here, in the garden.

Rain

When it rains,
I smile inside
knowing that
it will water
the flowers
in my heart.

Fireflies

On a dark night,
I borrowed little stars
from my garden and
put them in a jar
with tiny holes in the lid.
They looked like
a strand of glimmer lights.

I put them on the table
as a centerpiece of the
night garden so I could
watch them take turns
flickering on and off
for my amusement.

Then, I let them go free
so the dark night
wouldn't be lonely.

What Star Is This?

On a cloudless night
I can see a bright star
hanging low.
I'm not sure if
it is the North Star
but I like the way
it glows…

Brighter than the other
stars, it seems
as though it is within reach
for me to scoop up
with my hands…

I've seen it every night
for a week without fail.
It willfully prevails
over the other stars.
This star helps me
to know that some things
don't change
no matter what life brings;
the stars still radiate.

Indigo Sky

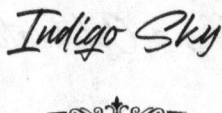

Moments after the sunset kissed
the line of the horizon good night
a darkling indigo blue sky emerged.
It left behind
several shades of vibrant blues.
This phenomenon must be
a one in a million sight.
The clouds look like bluebells
huddled together.
I was melancholy
until the sky's charm
surrounded me.

Life's a Celebration

The past has no
opportunity for
a second chance.
The past makes
you a little older
every day…so,
live each day
as if it's your
birthday!
Celebrate life
in some special way
each passing day!

The Rainbow

The misty water droplets
transform into an
elaborate rainbow
that may inspire someone
beneath its arch
to dance in the rain
and dream of a medley of colors.

The Pot of Gold

I used to chase
rainbows as a
four-year-old child
looking for the pot
of gold at the end
of the rainbow.
My mother had
the face and voice
of an angel so I had
no reason to disregard
her stories as false.

Although, I'm older now
I still chase after
rainbows that may have
a pot of gold.
The rainbows usually
end in the ocean,
lake, valley, or mountain.
I'm eager to see the
rainbow after a storm…
It reminds me that
good things are yet

to come.
It also reminds me to treasure
God's gifts, which are
more valuable than gold!

An Explorer

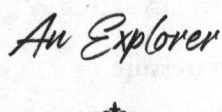

I explore the world
through the guests that stay at my inn.
They have been to many places
I haven't been to, seen things
I haven't seen, tasted delicacies
that haven't yet arrived on my plate.

They've visited castles,
and B&Bs,
seen active volcanoes,
taken the road to Hana,
bathed in the Blue Lagoon in Iceland,
taken a hot air balloon ride over a river,
swam with sharks in the depths of the ocean,
and whale watched while on a cruise;
all places I have yet to visit.

They've strolled in Paris for a day,
seen the Northern Lights,
traveled across country in an RV,
swam in the Bioluminescent Bay
at night in the Cayman Islands and
visited the exotic island of Mauritius.

They tell me stories of their travels.
I feel like I've explored the entire world
without actually leaving the inn!

Breathtaking

The sunset turned the
sky from ocean blue to peach,
pink, rose and then to a rust hue.

The Sun took a deep breath
and dove into the ocean.

Breathtaking…

My eyes inhale the
awesome sight.
I wait for the sun to exhale
to see the sunrise
in the early morning.

Summon Spring

I demand spring
appear!
It has been a
long deceitful
winter and spring
should be near...

When I thought
it was over
it wasn't
at all!
Summon spring, I say,
This is the last call!

The Minnesota
weather
is confused!
Shall it thaw,
snow, or rain?
The sun shines
on the edge of
the windowpane
as if it were a lasting
photograph.

Shall I write
spring's epitaph?
Where has it gone?
I pray that I'm wrong
and for tulips to appear
tomorrow, my dear.

Royal Tea

I live in a castle
where I can be queen.
I feel like royalty
when sipping on
tea and eating scones
with clotted-cream
and lemon curd.
I often dream of
having my own Royal Ball
where I'd dance all night
in a fancy dress
and think of nothing else at all!
Oh, the things I imagine
while sipping on Royal Tea!

Recipe of Love

A teaspoon of sugar
to sweeten your words
adds a pinch of kindness
that will surely go a long way.
Don't forget a fistful of kisses
blown into the mix
and let it sit for a while
to rise up in love like yeast in bread.
Oh, how love likes to grow
if given the right ingredients.

Smiles

When I'm exhausted
at night I
retreat to my room
on the third floor.
I'll rest
my head
on a soft cloud
and stare out
the window
to see the
smiling moon.
I smile back in return.

Alarm Clock

In the early morning,
the little ball
of orange fur
senses my eyes
are about to open.
She scampers about
my room before
jumping and lying
on my face
while she purrs
until I wake up and
swipe her off my face.
I touch the snooze button.
She returns twice more
before I'm fully awake for the day.
It's her duty!

Winter Cardinals

Almost every
winter day
I look out of
my large
office window
by my desk
and spy on the
bright red cardinals,
as if I'm incognito.

They rest there during
the afternoon, while
eating the bark
of the branches
of the tall bushes
that I failed to trim
over the summer.

I don't seem to bother
them when my curious
eyes meet their valiant
eyes.
How do they know
I don't want to eat them?

The "redbirds" look like
little balloons lifting
off when their
ravenous bellies
are full.
The females are
ethereal flowers.

It amazes me.
They stick around
all winter long,
but maybe it
is to put a smile
on my face.

They help me forget
the sting of the
cool, crisp air
and they brighten
the day in such a way
that makes life a little
easier…if they can make
it through the cold winter,
so can I!

Life Is a Poem

Living life on purpose
is a poetic action.
From the moment
you wake up to
a beautiful sunrise,
to the moment the
sun goes down…
and everything in
between is poetic.
The blue skies,
the birds singing.
It's like seeing
God's radiant love in disguise
and writing your best thoughts
on paper.
Green grass smashed
beneath your tiny feet
and listening to the
rhythm of your own heart beat.
All are poetic details
of your daily life.
Life is a poem!

Swans of the Lake

Lovers rule the lake
from dawn to dusk.
Their perfect silhouette
and graceful movements align
with the warm
beaming ray of sunshine
and the moonlit path.
When they kiss,
you can see an outline
of a heart that renders
their love for one another.

The swans of the lake
swim off into the
horizon
as they become
one with the earth.

Lilacs

Your light purple
delicate petals
send off a desirable
scent that meanders
through the fresh spring air.

While inhaling your
gift to humanity,
I admire your simplicity.

Red Roses

Elegant red roses
from the garden
will start a romance
in your heart
as you desire to
pick them for the
dining room table.

Regret

I wish regret
and I had never met!
It's impossible to
take back the past.
I wish these
dreadful memories
wouldn't last…
I wish regret was a dandelion
departing on a breeze
I would make a wish
to create new
joyful memories
to replace my regrets
so, take them away,
oh please!

A Midnight Visitor

As I toss and turn,
the rain tap dances
on my windowpane
in a gentle rhythmic fashion
as I doze in and out of sleep.

It's the best time for me
to fall asleep—
in the presence of
the soothing
sound of falling rain.

I'm glad the rain
stopped by to sing me a lullaby
at the midnight hour.

The Ocean Remembers

The ocean waves have
stashed away
millions of
lovely messages.
Written in the
sandy beaches
all around
the world,
the messages now
belong to the sea.

The written memos
are of peace
and love.
The messages
do not leave
anyone feeling lonely.

The ocean carries
these sandy notes
on waves from
island to island,
sea to sea,

shore to shore,
and have become
the heart of the
ocean...

Some say,
"Will you marry me?"
"I love you!"
or it could be as
simple as a name
drawn in the
wet sand
by a foot or a stick.

They were written
by honeymooners,
lovebirds, old
and young souls.

Many may forget
these messages
but the ocean will
always remember!

Chasing the Sun

My sissy chooses
to walk along
Seven-Mile Beach
in the Cayman Islands
alone early in
the morning.
She wants to see the rising sun,
to fulfill her desire
to be one
with the earth and sea
for a few hours.

It's as though she
has been chasing
the sun all her life,
so as not to miss
God's beautiful
creations.

Her heart beats
faster when
rushing to see
as it rises amongst

the ocean's
horizon line,
because no
two sunrises
are the same.

Maybe one day
she will see the
rising sun within her.
She, too, is unique!

A Cat's Melody

When I fall asleep
at night,
my kitten comes
into my room.
She opens the bedroom door
by herself with her thumbs.
She plops herself
on my chest
under my chin
as if she's a violin…
She'll sleep there all night
and purrs happiness until it's light.
She doesn't mind
that I snore
because to her,
I'm another cat
purring loudly.
Together, we
sing a lullaby
all night long.

Perennials

Perennials are
my true friends.
They visit
me again and again.
As long as I have
a garden to tend.

Annuals

Who frightened
the annuals
so they only
stay for one year?

Was it the lack
of attention…
water, sun, or
visitors?

Please come back
to my garden
and fill it with
your beauty!

Oh, how I miss them.
Sunflowers,
dahlias, begonias
and cosmos.
They all suddenly
had to go.

Red Velvet

A red velvet
rose is the
heart of my
garden,
which
beats strongly
for love.

Fields of Flowers

I dreamed of wildflowers…

A rainbow exploded
and left behind
fragments of colors
everywhere!

Scent of Lilacs

When I'm in
the presence
of my
purple lilacs,
I imagine
bottling its
sweet scent.
I'd treasure it
like an
exorbitant perfume
and wear it
every day,
so others
could smell
a waft of
heaven.

A New Year

May this year
be a little brighter;
may I remind
myself that
I am not weak
but a fighter!

May I dig
inside my heart
and find that
happiness was
there
all along…

May I learn
silly lyrics to a
new gospel song
to calm me
when I get
frustrated…

May I realize
that money is

overrated
and it's
happiness
that grows
and spreads.

May I realize that
all tangible things
have no heartbeat;
they're all dead.

I'm Ready

I'm ready for spring!

I'm ready for
new life to begin…

Spring flowers
and warm showers.

Mud puddles,
melted icicles
taking the
place of
bird baths.

I'm ready for
verdant growth
peeking through
the cold, dead earth.

The birds singing
a spring awakening
in the early mornings.

I'm ready for
budding trees
and a warm
spring breeze.

I'm ready for spring!

When Life Gives Me Lemons

When life is sour
I'm determined
to be the sugar
and compliment
someone
to sweeten
their day
and mine.

Gems of the Northern Minnesota Sky

The North Star
and the Northern
Lights illuminate
Minnesota's
night sky.

The stellar aurora
is an incredible
sight to see.

Most of the time,
the lights are a vibrant
emerald green,
ruby red,
yellow topaz,
blue sapphire,
turquoise,
a violet amethyst,
or purple tanzanite—
other colors can also
be spotted.

These colors stretch,
dance and leap
across the night sky
and form various
shapes that can fly.

Although
they are the colors
of gemstones,
their value far
outweighs real
quintessential gems,
earthly stars.

These sumptuous
gems of the sky
turn into forever memories
stored in our minds.

The February Sky

The Snow-Moon
is a giant night-light
illuminating the sky
on this frigid
February day.
Like a large
ivory marble
suspended from
the black velvet sky,
it gives us light
on the darkest
of nights.

The stars look like
small jacks
and the planets
seem to be marbles
shimmering
in the moonlight.

The stars and moon are scattered
and tossed into the evening sky,
by God for the enjoyment of our eyes.

Turning Colors

Spring is like
a chameleon changing
colors from
brown to green.

Summer changes colors
with droplets of dewy mist,
creating a rainbow of
colorful flowers.

Fall changes from blue skies
to colors of a brilliant sunset—
of bright florid color,
orange and gold.

Winter changes from
silvery frost on
dead leaves
to the whitest of snow.

Hot Air Balloon Rides in Stillwater

The best time for
hot air balloon rides
aloft the St. Croix River
is during the fall,
so you can see the
changing colors of the leaves.

Each balloon is dighted
in vibrant colors or patterns...
roaming the sky aimlessly
as it floats by.

Each leaf blowing
in the wind
tries to reach
astronomical heights—
the balloon at its peak...
as if it were a contest
to rule the skies.

Sipping on Memories

Pumpkin lattes,
Peruvian hot chocolate,
caramel apple cider,
my mother's eggnog,
royal Thai tea,
Auntie Myra's
hot buttered rum
or licorice tea
are all vivid
liquid memories.

It takes me back
to cozy
autumn days
or snowy, cold
winter nights.
Nostalgic.

Frozen Stars

The lucid
falling snowflakes
look like small twinkling
stars in the moonlight.

These falling stars
gracefully cover
the ground
and form a thin
layer of sparkles
that glisten in the
dark, quiet night.

Not for Sale

What's made
with
love is not
for sale!

Granny will
never sell her
delicious caramel-
cinnamon rolls
but she will
freely give me
the recipe and
teach me how
to make them.

What's made
with
love is not
for sale!

The Painting

It caught my eye
at the first glance.
I stared at its
brush strokes for
five minutes.
Although it was
incredibly simple,
vivacious even,
vegetables and lilies
leaped out
from the dark.
It had a black and green
background;
it was incredibly
simple.

I bought it at
an estate sale
for fifty dollars.
I thought it was
a print—a glaise,
until I looked
more closely

in the
bottom right
corner
by the faint
minuscule
signature.

That's where I found a
small grey hair
stuck in the
oil painting.
Was it a
fragment
of the artist's DNA?
Was it a hair from
the paintbrush?

The hair
authenticated it.
The painting was old
but stunning.
It was a
lovely surprise!
Now it hangs
in the parlor
for all the guests to see
and appreciate
an authentic piece of art.

The Last Snowflake to Fall

Now that winter is officially here
I've seen enough frozen tears
to cover the ground in white—
from those who have had enough
snow that has fallen night after night.
But the brazen winters make one tough…

The scintillating night's falling snow
continues to twinkle and glow
in the path of the moonlight
that surrounds the streetlights.
By the end of January, I'm ready to go…
I've seen enough of the cold powdered snow.
Winter, you must leave, so pack up and go!
Take with you all the fluffy white snow,
and wait for next winter's beckoning snow call.
I'm ready for winter to end and the last snowflake to fall.

Trumpeters on the St. Croix River

Their lush bodies resemble
little white sailboats gliding
across the mirrored, vitreous water
gleaming with variegated leaves
and a golden wheat sun.

Their swagged necks
dive in the water
in search of an easy meal
of foliage on this clear
autumn day…

Although bottoms are in the air,
they still look like the most
elegant and graceful birds
ever seen.

Fall in Love Again at the Inn

To fall in love is a miracle of two hearts
beating to the same rhythm.

When I see two people in love at the inn,
my heart smiles and I'm reminded
true love definitely exists.

Whether they're married for two years
or twenty, I see the same sparkle in their eyes
as if they fell in love again at the inn.

A Dandelion Tale
(Weed or Flower?)

I'm a dandelion that was chopped into pieces by a lawnmower...as if my future wishes don't mean a thing.

I will grow back brighter than the sun someday. For some ignore my beauty and think I'm a weed; I have a purpose.

The bees love me and make sweet honey, for they know my true value.

A Rosy Cheek

I remember trying to dodge your
perfect lips a thousand times
as a young child.
Now, I surrender and let
your puckered lips stain
my cheek with
a red impression
in the shape of a rose.

Your love of red roses
are seen in all you say
and do…
You smile often
when you see a dozen
red roses in the middle
of your kitchen table;
they smile back at you…
Although yellow, white,
and pink roses reside in your garden,
I know it's the red rose you favor.
To you, it smells the best
and it leans toward you
as if you were the sun.

Oh, how your face lights up,
when someone gives you
a large red rose.

Whenever I see a red rose,
I will forever remember
your sweet, loving kiss…
that resulted in a rosy cheek!

Thank you, Granny,
for sharing your love
amidst your radiant bliss!

Dreams

Dreams are like moving clouds in the sky.
They must push forward for you
to see the sun.

They're like a sunburst peeking through
trying to allure you
to each dream, a different shape
which may be in reach…

But a dream deferred will become
a thing of the past
if you don't embrace it
and believe in yourself.

So, dream a thousand dreams
and thousands more
to increase your chances
of at least one coming true.

Yes, it can happen to you!

A Broken Wing

I may have a broken wing
but I can still gladly sing…

I will sing louder than before
about all the things I adore.

Give praise to Him
for healing and not giving up
on an old songbird.

I'll sing songs of pure bliss
although the wing was badly
torn apart by my enemy.

The broken wing made me sing
a new song of hope,
heard in my voice.

I may fly again
one happy day
and soar towards
the billowing clouds;
I'll fly towards the heights of a bright future.

Someone said,
"I couldn't and wouldn't
ever fly again…"
That I would never be the same.
They tried to drown me in
guilt and shame…
Because they didn't know
that I could heal and certainly fly
from the one who knows my name.

God heard my song, a battle cry.
He heard my praise from heaven—a sweet song
and He told me all my critics were wrong
to sing louder than before
and flap my wings harder
as they lifted me off the floor.

I will thank God for my broken wing
all glory to the one
who taught me how to grow and sing.
He's the one who gave me strength within,
that came from a valiant king.
When I thought I couldn't sing,
He had plans to mend my wing
and help me sing louder than before
and it swooped me off the floor.

From the bottom of my heart's core,
I thank you God for helping me
realize I could sing
when everyone else was
focused on my broken wing!

Blooming Passionflower

If I were a flower
I'd be an exotic
passionflower.
It exudes the scent of joy.

It leans with the wind
and lets the
water droplets
roll off its petals
as if not to disturb
creation itself.

Its color
is that of royalty,
a deep purple,
when fully in bloom.
Its beauty is uniquely
put together, having
many distinct parts
as it produces the
passion fruit.

This flower
attracts an audience.
If I were a passionflower,
I'd grow in a lovely garden
in Samara, Costa Rica
and greet the bees and butterflies
with a smile every day.

Maple Tree Row

I walked through Maple Tree Row.

The leaves above
caught my thirsty eyes
and filled them with awe
as I marveled
at the sight of
Maple Tree Row.
Tree after tree,
growing in harmony
on each side of
the winding path.

Hiking here
for the first time,
I realize
the calmness of
this moment
belongs to the
space and time
of autumn.

A fall color
of bright fire
rules this forest.
It makes
me stop and look
all around
because of its surrealness.

I can't see the
sugared sap inside
the maple tree
but I know it is there.

An invisible wind
blows the leaves
around on the ground.
The sap is
the soul of the maple tree.
These pleasing souls
of the forest
make life a little
sweeter in autumn!

Bittersweet Is Hidden in My Heart

As fall weddings warm
the air with love,
bittersweet vines warm
fall's crisp air
with its stunning beauty…

Its plump, bright orange
berries hang from
curling vines that
wrap around trees.

From a distance,
a bundle resembles
a bunch of thin twigs
or grapevines,
but its beauty is hidden.

The Best Present

Love is a little package
wrapped in a heart
with a bow of heart strings
attached and given
to a person without
expecting a gift in return.

A Winter Reverie

It's a foggy November day.
The rain is but
a mist
and I'm making
a mental list
of all the flowers
I can plant in spring
to attract butterfly wings.

I envision a butterfly garden
in my backyard by the
cement bird bath
tucked away by
the purple
lilac bushes.
It will be colorful
and sweetly scented.

I imagine hiring a gardener
who will know
all the flowers
by their fancy names:
hollyhock,

globe centaurea,
zinnias,
rock cress,
and nasturtium.

We'll also plant wildflowers,
such as
yellow blazing stars,
that will shine
two feet high,
towering over
the butterfly sky.

All the flowers will attract
notable guests:
monarchs,
harvesters,
giant swallowtails,
hackberry emperors,
white admirals,
mourning cloaks,
blues and skippers.

Each butterfly will flit
from flower to flower,
drunk with nectar.

The butterfly garden
will be organic—

free from pesticides.
Some weeds
will grow and attract
more butterflies
to distract our eyes
from blue skies.

And with a prayer,
God will
command
the wind
to be still
and the butterflies
won't worry
about
crash landings.

The small plot of land
will be exposed to
the sun's rays
and give the
garden life
and energy.

I'll daydream
of the next spring
or summer
that will fly by on
butterfly wings.

Making Friends

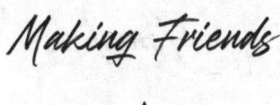

A cheerful giggle in your voice
Make a new friend by choice

Quick as a wink to impress
Lose the aimless distress

Learn something new
to see how your connection grew

Tall above the flowers
Know another might cower

Instead of stretching…
skip compliment fetching.

And be as real as can be
so, they'll all see

We all connect
when we are direct

Charm
without harm
Make a new friend!

Honey

I watch the busy
bees buzz around
my garden
and wonder
how a creature
who can sting
manages to make such
sweet honey?

Then, I'm reminded
the bee isn't any
different than a human
who can sting with
their little tongue
by untactful word choices.
They can *choose* to
produce words
that leave the taste
of honey on their lips
and sweet music
in your ears,
but they won't always do so.

Solo Bird

Every day I see the same
bird hanging on the
telephone wire
all by himself
in front of my house.
He doesn't twitter—
he makes no sound.

Why doesn't he have a flock?
I wonder.
Is he searching for a mate?
Did his mate die and
he vowed never to love again.

All sorts of scenarios
run through my mind.
For now, his name is Solo Bird.

Spring

The tulips spring forward
with bursts of colors everywhere!

The moss is a vibrant green
spreading joy across the garden floor.

The sweet smell of fragrant cherry blossoms
reach the depths of my nostrils.

I can almost taste the morel mushrooms
sizzling in a pan with butter.

I hear the rain fall gently,
as if it doesn't want to wake
the garden until the sun comes out.

Spring is here; the snow has melted away.
Children have come out to play!

A Lovely Red Rose

I'm a red rose
planted by
the garden's gate.
Hurry, don't wait…
Love at first glance.
Don't miss your chance.
Pick me and lift me to your nose.
Something is special about
a blooming red rose.
My scent is like no other.
You'll certainly not fall in love
with another.

Seeds

Plant seeds of
beautiful wildflowers
throughout the garden.

Wait for the wind to blow
and the sun to surely glow
for the rain to show.

The seeds will exemplify a rainbow,
but instead of in the sky,
they'll beam for a passerby.

Plant seeds of
beautiful wildflowers
throughout the garden.

Duckling Crossing

The fuzzy yellow ducklings
wobble as they follow
their mother across
the busy road
to their destination—
a nearby lake, where they will mature
for the next two months.
They don't look both ways…
Cars slam on their brakes.
Some drivers swear under their breath
for being inconvenienced
as they wait for the ducklings to cross.
I'm in the car waiting patiently
and the ducklings remind me
that spring is finally here!
I've been waiting all year.
So, if I have to wait a
few more minutes,
I'll sit back and
watch the bird show…
It doesn't bother me to know
that life is full of little surprises,
even on the road that leads one
to see spring begin again!

Not Long Ago

Not long ago,
we attended
concerts, weddings,
music in the park,
and traveled abroad.

Now, we stay at home
and hide under our masks,
a smile now is a nod.

We appreciate what
we have in our own
towns and cities…

We no longer care if
our faces look pretty;
we sleep in and stay
six feet apart.
We fear going to the store
and touching dirty carts.

We wait for the pandemic
to pass like a slow-moving fog…
We find excuses to get out
and walk our little dogs.

We long to breathe fresh,
untainted air.
We want to return
to the workplace and
cut our hair!

We took such things for granted.
Now, we try to bloom where we're planted.
We wish we could freely do these things
that seem to have a lot of worth…
If I could, I would grow wings
and I'd fly away from this stricken earth.

Summer Sky

Soon it will be summer
and I'll lay in the grass
at night. I'll aim my eyes
for the stars and let them
wander to the moon and back.
I will focus
on the twinkling stars from
where I lay in the garden.
It reminds
me that the Summer Sky
has surely arrived in heaven.

Green Grass

Fresh, clean and damp
beneath my bare feet.
I'm happy that we
did meet
on such
an occasion as
this.
My toes curl in the
green grass—
pure love and bliss!

Freedom Flower

I dreamt I was an exhilarating sunflower
stretching tall beneath the sunrise
in the early morning of the month of July.
The pleasure of freedom-waving petals in the wind
like the American flag attached to my house.

Heartbeats

When I marry again,
I'll treasure our time
together.
It will be
measured by
heartbeats united
instead of seconds.

Peru's Rainbow Mountain

This is one of the only places
on Earth where you can
climb upon a rainbow.
The different shades of sediment
leave behind a variety of colors
on the mountain top
in rows or strips of earth.
This place is celestial…
If you drank all the
morning mountain's dew,
you would sparkle like the sun
and radiate like a rainbow, too!

Morning Sunshine

If I could capture a sun's ray,
I'd put it in my morning
coffee cup so I could
beam of light in
someone's life
all day long!

Summer Symphony

I hear the grasshopper
rub his legs together.
Dragonflies are little
helicopters humming
above the flower-tops.
Bees buzz by as they
fly from flower
to flower.
Songbirds chime in with
a melodious love song.
Romeo, the frog,
sunbathes on a lily pad,
croaking vehemently.
Hummingbirds zoom by
the daylilies and hollyhocks.
The garden is a Broadway stage
featuring a vivacious symphony!

Love Each Other

When your face lights up, so does mine!
When my face lights up, so does yours!
This is how I know we truly love each other!

When I'm sad, you're sad.
When you're sad, I'm sad.
That is how I know we truly love each other!

Lily Pads

Delicate lily pads float along the lake
sitting still, careful not to break.

Lily pads wait for visitors
to make themselves at home.

Beneath their wings,
they hide and protect fish.

They wait for frogs
that haven't yet been kissed
to hitch a ride.

Sunflower

Be a towering sunflower
that blooms among the weeds
and outshines the sun.

Dance Like the Earth

Dance like the rain; it's refreshing!
Dance like the wind; it's powerful!
Dance like the current; it's free flowing!

A Rose in a Teacup

There's a pink rose in my teacup…
simply floating and blooming there.
Lonely, it is not…as I delightfully stare.
It's a Victorian Beauty, lovely and rare
swimming in my teacup.
Placed by someone
who thoughtfully put it there.
It brings a smile to my face
to help me forget fruitless cares.
Now, it's easier to breathe in
its sweet-scented crisp air
because someone had a heart
and a pink rose to spare.

Dear Reader,

Below are my favorite life quotes. I hope you will be inspired by the words and enjoy them.

—*Rachelle N. Rose*

"Continue to dream in a world of opportunities. If you stop dreaming, so will the world!"

"Don't forget to love yourself a little more each day and soon you'll be filled with love to full capacity."

"Love wins every battle!"

"Toxic people pollute the world wherever they go."

"Kind people leave trails of goodness wherever they go."

"Love cancels hate…in fact, it squashes it to death!"

"Catchy tunes etch a pathway to your heart so be careful what you listen to."

"Leave your smile as your signature so no one will be able to forge it!"

"Wrinkles from laughter are the best type of wrinkles. They turn up at the ends to create smiles."

"Say, 'Hi!' to strangers with a smile; you may be the only sunshine they see all day!"

"Try loving without words; actions are stronger anyhow!"

"Live life on purpose and your purpose will be revealed to you."

"Hugs fill the world with love and compassion; hug long and hold on tight."

"Love to love, hate to hate."

"When the sky cries, its tears nourish the ground."

"Dolphins are angels of the sea."

"Smile on purpose."

"Sad faces have the most wrinkles."

"Be joyful and you'll stay young; your heart never ages."

"Dear sister, you have a voice, now go be heard!"

"I have several reasons to be just me!"

"Negativity and worldly things eat away the outer edges of your soul, but positivity builds a wall around it that the enemy can't tear down."

"Don't let your past define you!"

"To ignore justice is to back-peddle. It gets us nowhere. To embrace justice is to move forward with progress."

"There is no such thing as loving too little but there is such a thing as loving or caring too little."

"Equip yourself with the tools to bury the past!"

"Some say love is a game that can't be won!"

"I never met a poet who didn't write of love. Love is a necessity…without it, we will shrivel up and die like a red rose without water. When we love we bloom and emit a sweet fragrance."

"If love were a flower, I'd send you fields and fields of wildflowers to remind you of my love for you!"

"If you're running on empty, you're decaf."

About the Author

Rachelle Nevaeh Rose grew up in historic Stillwater, Minnesota. She has always loved to write and stretch her vivid imagination. As a child, she learned that writing was very rewarding; describing things in a way that gets someone's attention has fueled her love to write.

She graduated from the College of St. Catherine in St. Paul with a B.S. in Education. She has pursued one of her dreams and purchased a bed and breakfast in the summer of 2017, Aurora Staples Inn, which is located in Stillwater. She enjoys writing a poetry column for <u>Bed and Breakfast Magazine</u>, loves to travel, read, go to the gym, run, salsa dance, hike, Zumba and cook.

www.ingramcontent.com/pod-product-compliance
Lightning Source LLC
Chambersburg PA
CBHW012106090526
44592CB00019B/2669